Homework Tonight

With Answers

Book 2

Kim Stewart

Illustrated by Jan Wade

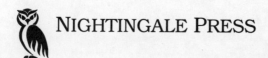

Australia   NIGHTINGALE PRESS   United Kingdom

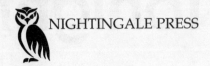

NIGHTINGALE PRESS

Devised and produced by:
NIGHTINGALE PRESS,
UNIT 350, GLENFIELD PARK SITE 2,
BLAKEWATER ROAD
BLACKBURN, LANCASHIRE BB1 5QH

This edition produced in 1996 for Pegasus Distribution LTD.,
UNIT 350, GLENFIELD PARK SITE 2,
BLAKEWATER ROAD
BLACKBURN, LANCASHIRE BB1 5QH

Editor Consultant: Brenda Apsley
Illustrator: Jan Wade

Printed in Australia

ISBN 1 875 288 54 6
ISBN 1 875288 52 X Set

About this book

Effective learning comes as the result of a three-way partnership between child, parent and teacher in a learning environment that combines home, school and the outside world.

Homework Tonight is a series of six books, specially designed for use at home, that will build on, support and reinforce your child's work. The series covers all three National Curriculum core subjects English, Mathematics and Science and Technology to Key Stage 1 and Key Stage 2.

Each **Homework Tonight** book provides 30 carefully structured homework units, each unit providing a stimulating mix of topics that include:
- Reading, writing and comprehension exercises
- Spelling guides and practice exercises
- Word usage, grammar and punctuation exercises
- Mathematics exercises including number work, measurement, shape and space
- Handwriting practise
- Research, and information gathering

The units are designed to be 'self guiding', but you should offer help whenever it is needed. You may need to read instructions with your child and explain basic concepts. Answers are provided at the back of each book.

Make homework a regular part of your child's life. The progression of work is carefully structured, so encourage your child to work through the units beginning at 1 and ending at 30. Aim to complete a unit per day, or per week - whatever is right for your child.

As you work through each unit with your child, offer help and encouragement. Praise effort, and do not criticise a ' wrong ' answer. Adopt a positive attitude. Rather than pointing out ' mistakes ', encourage your child to try working through problem areas again, with your help and guidance. Do not enforce homework as a chore or punishment; instead, make it a fun, shared experience that your child will look forward to. Help your child to develop a pride in producing good work, and extend some of the activities, for example by colouring pictures, reading more widely about a topic or devising additional maths activities. Always remember that you are your child's favourite teacher.

Encourage a sense of progress and achievement by checking, then ticking or signing each unit as it is completed, and don't forget to fill in the certificate of achievement on page 70. You may also like to award gold stars or 'well done' stickers for work of a very high standard.

No two children are alike. No two children learn in the same way or at the same pace. You know your child best. Work at a level and speed that suits him or her, and make homework an invaluable part of the learning partnership.

SPACE

Find a similar shape in a magazine. Cut it out and paste in.

MEASUREMENT

Draw a dinosaur taller than the tree.

NUMBER

Draw extra suns to make 9.

SPELLING

Add these letters to **at**.

___ at

___ at   ___ at

___ at

___ at

___ at

___ at

___ at

c p
h b m
r f
s

Write a sentence using some **at** words.

HANDWRITING

l i

Trace

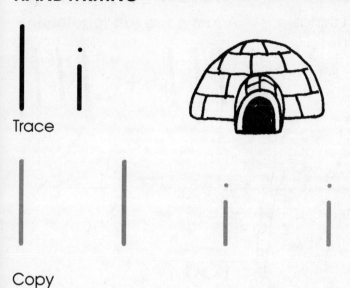

l l i i

Copy

READING

Draw a hand holding the ice lolly. Draw a plate under it.

i
i i
i i
i
i

How many i letters are dripping from the ice lolly? _____

ENGLISH

I can draw my...

eyes

nose

hair

ears

mouth

eyebrows

Child's Name	Parent's Signature

SPACE

Make a pattern down the page using these shapes. Make it a 2 colour pattern.

MEASUREMENT

Colour the rough things. Circle the smooth.

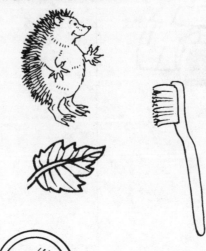

NUMBER

Add the two sets together.

= _____

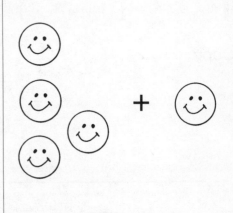

= _____

SPELLING

Fill the net with **et** words.

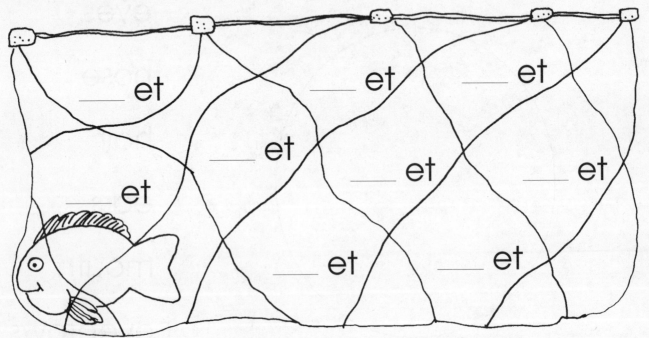

___ et

___ et

___ et

___ et

___ et

___ et

___ et

___ et

___ et

These letters will help you.

j   b   w   l   n   s   g   p   v

6

HANDWRITING

L l

Trace

L L l l

Copy

READING

Draw a duck on a pond. Put a frog on the bank.

ENGLISH

Unjumble these words.

duck   frog   pond   tree

eter   gofr   cudk   pndo

| Child's Name | Parent's Signature |

Unit 3

SPACE

Put a fence around the hen house. Put 3 chickens on the right side of the hen house. Put a pond in front.

MEASUREMENT

Draw a full bottle of drink. Draw a half filled glass of drink.

NUMBER

Colour the coins that fell out of the purse.

How many are left? _____

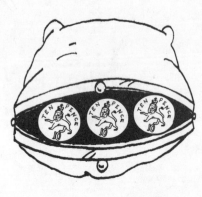

SPELLING

Help Grandma knit some **it** words.
These letters will help you.
s b f h k l

___ it

___ it

___ it

___ it

___ it

___ it

HANDWRITING

T t

Trace

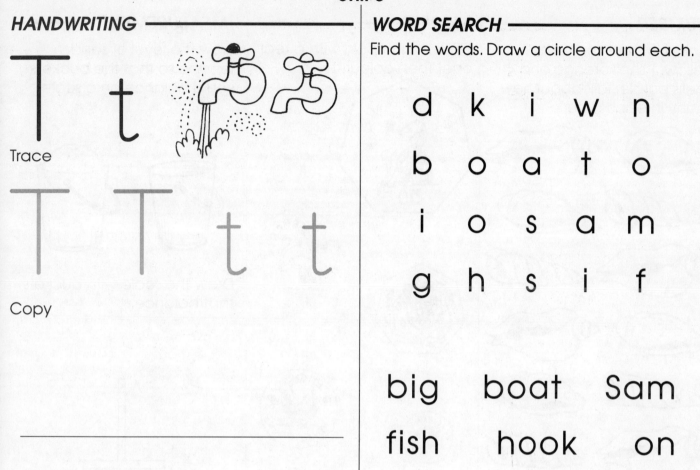

T T t t

Copy

_____

WORD SEARCH

Find the words. Draw a circle around each.

d k i w n
b o a t o
i o s a m
g h s i f

big   boat   Sam
fish   hook   on

READING

Sam caught a big fish on Saturday.

1. Who caught the fish? _____

2. On what day did he catch it? _____

3. How did Sam feel? _____

Child's Name	Parent's Signature

9

NUMBER

Colour 5 shells red, 2 shells yellow, 1 shell orange and 4 shells purple. Talk about how many in each group.

MONEY

Cover each coin with a real one. Then colour them.

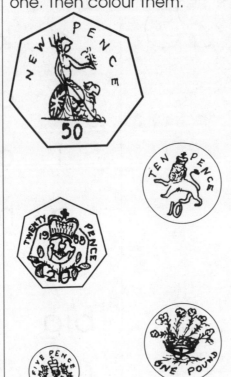

MEASUREMENT

Show the level of sand needed so that the buckets would balance on a scale.

Draw the scale with buckets that balance.

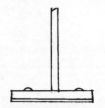

SPELLING

What goes into the pot?

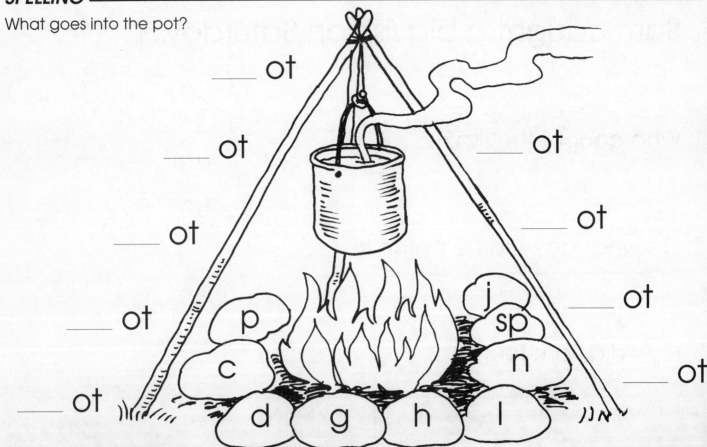

___ ot

___ ot

___ ot

___ ot

___ ot

j
sp
p
c
n
d g h l

___ ot

___ ot

___ ot

___ ot

HANDWRITING

J j

Trace

J J j j

Copy

J J j j

READING

Draw a tent near a river. Draw 2 children playing.

ENGLISH

Say the colours. Then colour each part of the caterpillar to match the words.

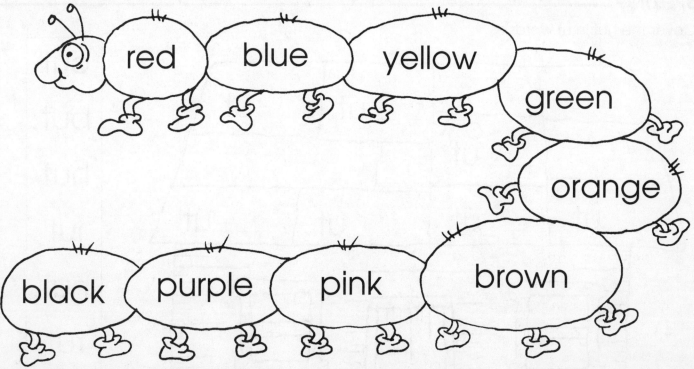

red   blue   yellow   green   orange

black   purple   pink   brown

Child's Name	Parent's Signature

Unit 5

Complete the patterns down the page.

MEASUREMENT

Write the days of the week in the correct order.

1. _____

2. _____

3. _____

4. _____

5. _____

6. _____

7. _____

Friday Wednesday
Sunday Tuesday
Saturday Monday
Thursday

NUMBER

How many birds are left when 2 fly away?

How many bees are left when 1 buzzes away?

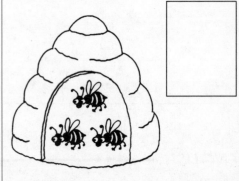

SPELLING

Cover the hut in **ut** words.

cut

but

hut

jut

nut

rut

put

12

HANDWRITING

U u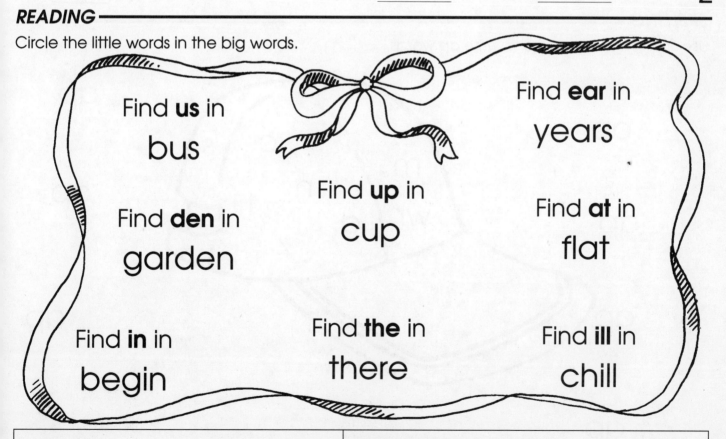

Trace

U

Copy

U U u u

_____

ALPHABET

Fill in the blanks to write the alphabet.

a _____ c _____

f g _____ _____

_____ l _____ o

_____ q _____

u _____ _____

_____ z

READING

Circle the little words in the big words.

Find **us** in
bus

Find **den** in
garden

Find **in** in
begin

Find **up** in
cup

Find **the** in
there

Find **ear** in
years

Find **at** in
flat

Find **ill** in
chill

Child's Name	*Parent's Signature*

Unit 6

SPACE

Colour the **left** sock blue.
Colour the **middle** sock green.

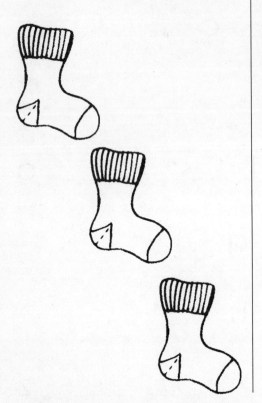

MEASUREMENT

Draw a picture of something you do on a weekday.

NUMBER

Colour the 20 pence coins red. How many are there?
Colour any 50 pence coins green. How many are there?

20p ☐   50p ☐

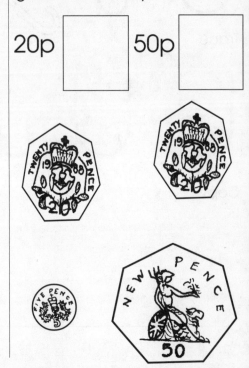

SPELLING

Use the letters in the cap to write **ap** words.

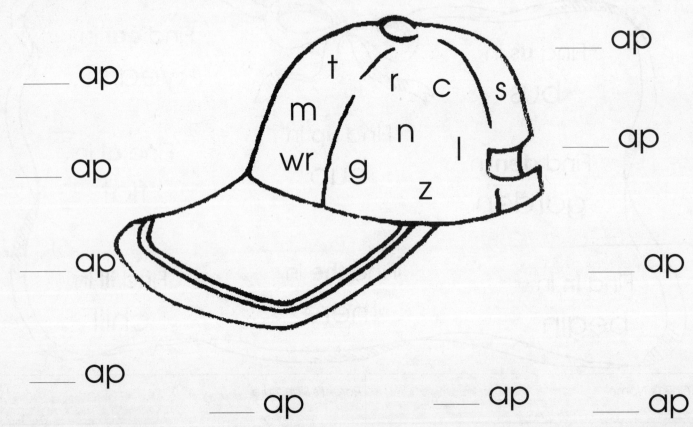

___ ap

___ ap

___ ap

___ ap

___ ap

___ ap

___ ap

___ ap

___ ap

14

HANDWRITING

Trace

Copy

ALPHABET

Put the words in alphabetical (a b c) order.

cake   1. _____

kite   2. _____

frog   3. _____

baby   4. _____

man   5. _____

egg   6. _____

READING

Join words and pictures.

sleep

draw

read

play

run

skip

Child's Name	Parent's Signature

15

Unit 7

SPACE

Colour circles for the number of boys and girls in your family.

(circles)

girls   boys

MEASUREMENT

Draw the thing you love doing most when you are hot.

NUMBER

Draw the total number of clocks.

+

= _____

WORD BUILDING

Write more words to match the top words.

bat	bet	bit	but	blot
___at	___et	___it	___ut	___ot
___at	___et	___it	___ut	___ot
___at	___et	___it	___ut	___ot

_____ _____ _____ _____ _____

16

HANDWRITING

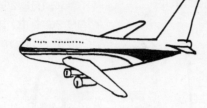

A a

Trace

A A a a

Copy

_____

SPELLING

Circle the words that have '**a**' in them.

axe	goat
box	sack
mix	nine
day	had
zoo	very
van	walk
yes	watch

READING AND WRITING

Complete these words.

___pple   ___gloo   bo___   ___ebra

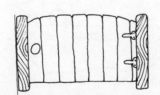
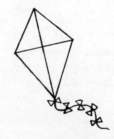

___eb   ___ate   ___ite   ___nake

Child's Name	*Parent's Signature*

PROBLEMS

What am I?
I am tall. I grow in the ground. I have a thick, rough trunk.

I live in the sea. I have a hard shell. I have 2 strong nippers.

MEASUREMENT

Draw a pattern on the longer ribbon.

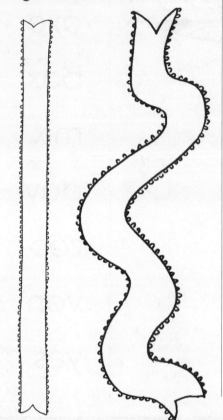

NUMBER

Trace the zero. Draw lines from the zero to the things that contain nothing.

SPELLING

Write the **ip** words.

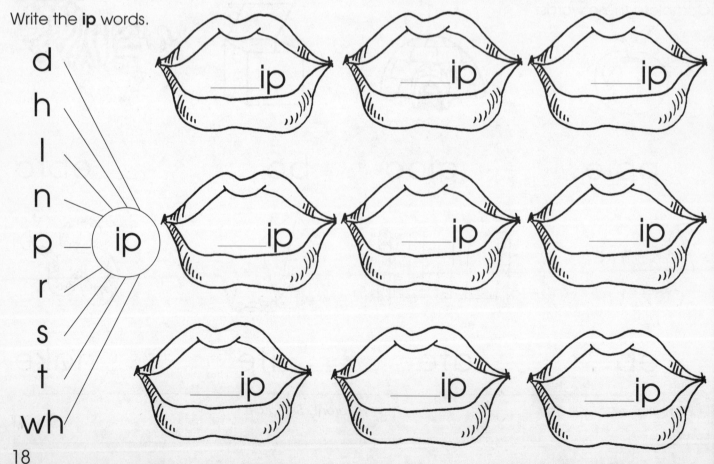

d
h
l
n
p
r
s
t
wh

ip

18

HANDWRITING

D d

Trace

D D d d

Copy

_____

ALPHABET

Fill in the blanks in the alphabet list.

1. a ___ ___ d e ___ ___

2. t ___ v ___ ___ ___

3. ___ m ___ ___ p ___

4. ___ ___ c ___ ___

5. f ___ ___ ___ ___ k

ENGLISH

Rewrite the sentences, putting in the capital letters and full stops.

1. josh went swimming in the lake

_____

2. ellen and jake had a birthday

_____

3. on sunday sam went to a party

_____

Child's Name	Parent's Signature

19

SPACE

Draw the symmetrical image of a lampshade.

MEASUREMENT

Colour the inside of this shape.

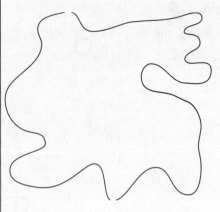

Draw a shape with curves.

NUMBER

Cut out 10 faces from a magazine. Paste them on a piece of paper. Trace the 10's.

Draw 10 stars.

SPELLING

Make as many **an** words as you can. You may be able to add extra sausages.

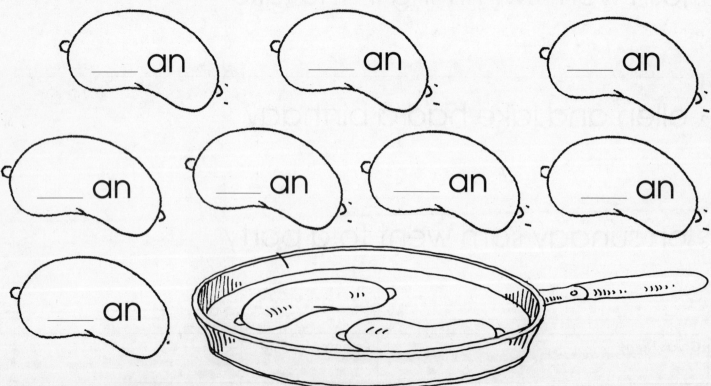

___an   ___an   ___an

___an   ___an   ___an   ___an

___an

HANDWRITING

G g

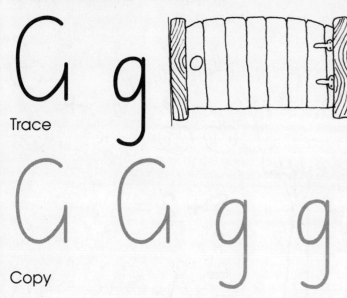

Trace

Copy

G G g g

READING

Find the hidden word.

1. Write the 2nd letter in shop.
2. Write the 4th letter in colour.
3. Write the 1st letter in middle.
4. Write the 3rd letter in green.
5. Write the 4th letter in brown.
6. Write the 5th letter in cannot.
7. Write the 1st letter in round.
8. Write the 5th letter in black.

1   2   3   4   5   6   7   8

ENGLISH

Right dog, left dog.

Put a pink bowl near the left dog.

Put a blue bowl near the right dog.

Give the left dog 3 black spots.

Give the right dog 3 orange spots.

Colour the dog on the left brown.

Colour the dog on the right yellow.

Give the dog on the left a red collar.

Give the dog on the right a green collar.

Child's Name	*Parent's Signature*

Unit 10

SPACE

Draw a shape that is rounded.

Draw a shape that is pointed.

MEASUREMENT

Draw a flower under the smallest tree. Draw a bird in the biggest tree.

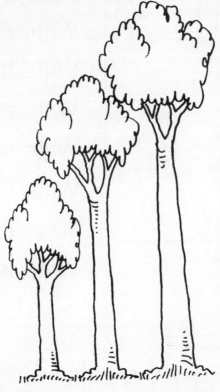

NUMBER

Addition.

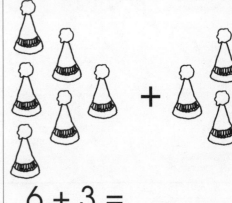

$5 + 2 =$ _____

$6 + 3 =$ _____

SPELLING

Add **en** to make some words.

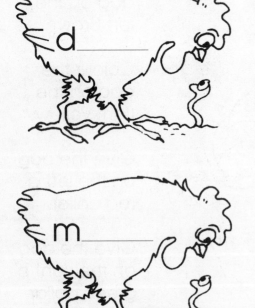

d_____

h_____

p_____

m_____

t_____

wh_____

22

HANDWRITING

Q q

Trace

Copy

Q Q q q

READING

I am a boy.
I am playing with a red car
and a green train.
Draw me.

WRITING

Write a story using these words.

sun   sand   beach   holiday

_____

_____

_____

_____

Child's Name	Parent's Signature

SPACE

Draw the reflection on the other side of the dotted line.

- - - - - - - - - - - - - -

MEASUREMENT

Name the heaviest person in your family.

_____

Name the lightest person in your family.

_____

Name something heavy in your bedroom.

_____

NUMBER

Cross off 5 hearts. How many left?

8 take away
5 leaves   _____

Cross off 2 flowers. How many left?

4 take away
2 leaves   _____

SPELLING

Write some more words to match.

f

p

w

sp

b

th

ch

(in)

1. _____   2. _____

3. _____   4. _____

5. _____   6. _____

7. _____

Draw a thin pin in the bottom of a bin.

24

HANDWRITING

C c

Trace

C C C C

Copy

_____

READING

Make 1 word from the 2 words. The first is done for you.

light + house = lighthouse

_____ + _____ = _____

_____ + _____ = _____

ENGLISH

Write the sentences in the correct order.

1. _____

2. _____

3. _____

4. _____

Throw line into water.
Tie a hook on your line.
Wait until you feel a bite.
Put bait on your hook.

Child's Name	Parent's Signature

25

MEASUREMENT

Circle the book that will take a long time to read.

Name 3 things that take a short time to do.

1. _____

2. _____

3. _____

NUMBER

How many things in each row?

 _____

 _____

2 rows of _____ = _____

Draw 3 rows of 4 objects.

SPELLING

Make the words by writing **un.**

 b_____

 f_____

 r_____

 n_____

 g_____

 s_____

HANDWRITING

O o

Trace

O O O O

Copy

ALPHABET

Write these words in alphabetical (abc) order.

1. Wednesday, Tuesday, Sunday, Monday

2. dog, fish, horse, cat

3. sand, water, crab, beach

ENGLISH

Punctuate the sentences by using capital letters and full stops. Remember, people's names have a capital. Write each sentence underneath.

1. glen, tim and dylan went sailing

2. andrew loves to play with his toys

3. my friends kathy and Lara came to play

Child's Name	Parent's Signature

MEASUREMENT

Find a pencil. List 3 things longer than the pencil.

1. _____

2. _____

3. _____

List 3 things shorter than the pencil.

1. _____

2. _____

3. _____

NUMBER

Colour half of each picture.

SPELLING

Read and draw these **bl** words.

blackboard

blanket

blackbird

blouse

HANDWRITING

E e

Trace

E E e e

Copy

_____

READING

Write an invitation for your birthday party.

Dear _____

Please come to my party.

When: _____

Where: _____

Time: _____

Please come.

From _____

ALPHABET

Draw pictures of these in alphabetical order.

book   shoe   car   glove

1

2

3

4

Child's Name	Parent's Signature

Unit 14

SPACE

Make a train like the one shown. Draw cylinders of different sizes.

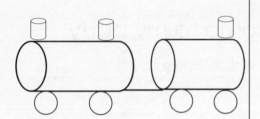

How many cylinders make up your train? _____

MEASUREMENT

Add a line to each shape to make it closed.

NUMBER

Write the numeral for how many in each bowl.

 _____

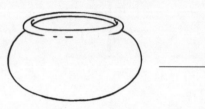 _____

 _____

SPELLING

Write the correct **cl** word under each picture. Use the word bank.

_____

_____

_____

_____

clap
clover
clown
clock
cloud

30

HANDWRITING

N n

Trace

N N n n

Copy

ALPHABET

Alphabetical order. Write:

1. The letter before c _____

2. The letter after t _____

3. The letter before r _____

4. The letter after w _____

5. The letter before o _____

Draw some things that start with **n.**

ENGLISH

Make a monster.

1. Draw 7 purple eyes.

2. Draw 3 more arms.

3. Draw 2 noses.

4. Give the monster green boots.

5. Draw 3 red mouths.

6. Give each mouth 4 blue teeth.

Child's Name	Parent's Signature

Unit 15

SPACE

Draw a line of symmetry through each of these shapes.

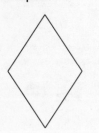

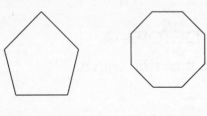
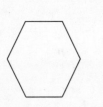

MEASUREMENT

Circle the bucket that will hold the greatest amount.

NUMBER

Write the numerals 0 - 10.

_____ _____ _____

_____ _____ _____

_____ _____ _____

_____

SPELLING

Add **sl** to these words.

__ __ ed

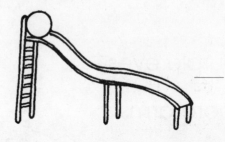

__ __ ide

__ __ ippers

__ __ eeve

__ __ eep

32

HANDWRITING

M m

Trace

M M mm

Copy

_____

WORD BUILDING

Write some words that mean the same as "big".

1. _____

2. _____

3. _____

4. _____

5. _____

READING

Read, then answer the questions.

On Saturday Natalie and Joseph built a big castle from red blocks.

Draw Natalie and Joseph building the castle.

1. What did Natalie and Joseph build?

_____

2. When did they build it?

_____

3. What colour was the castle?

_____

Child's Name	Parent's Signature

SPACE

Circle the things that will float.

MEASUREMENT

Colour the number of circles to make the scales balance.

Colour the number of circles to make the balance go down.

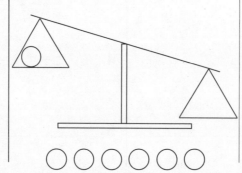

NUMBER

Complete these addition sums.

$5 + 2 = $ _____

$7 + 1 = $ _____

$9 + 0 = $ _____

$3 + 6 = $ _____

$4 + 4 = $ _____

$8 + 2 = $ _____

SPELLING

Write the correct word next to each picture.

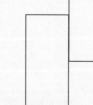

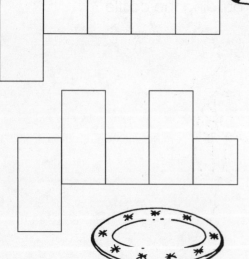

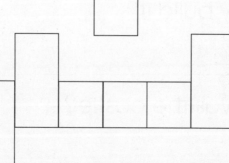

| plant | planet | plane | plate |

HANDWRITING

H h

Trace

H H H h h

Copy

WORD BUILDING

Write some words that begin with the letter "**h**".

1. _____

2. _____

3. _____

4. _____

5. _____

ENGLISH

Fill in the speech bubbles.

Child's name	Parent's Signature

MEASUREMENT

Name something that takes longer than...

1. Eating a bar of chocolate.

_____

2. Making your bed.

_____

3. Brushing your hair.

NUMBER

Complete these subtraction (take away) sums.

6 - 0 = _____

9 - 5 = _____

7 - 6 = _____

4 - 3 = _____

7 - 2 = _____

9 - 3 = _____

SPELLING

Colour the things in the shop that start with "s".

HANDWRITING

B b

Trace

B B b b

Copy

_____

READING

Circle the little words in the big words.

Find **at** in   mat

Find **to** in   into

Find **it** in   fit

Find **his** in   this

Find **ray** in   tray

Find **on** in   pond

Find **hop** in   shop

Find **eat** in   meat

ENGLISH

Unjumble the sentences and write them.

1. sat wall. Humpty on Dumpty a

_____

2. party. to going I am a

_____

3. watching Amy television. is

_____

Child's Name	Parent's Signature

NUMBER

Label these groups.

_____ groups of _____

_____ groups of _____

MEASUREMENT

Share the apples equally into the baskets.

SPELLING

Write the **th** words.

th — ree
in
ick
roat
ey
under

1. _____
2. _____
3. _____
4. _____
5. _____
6. _____

Circle the words that have **th** in them.

There once were three thin friends. They loved to play in the rain. Theo did not like the thunder.

BOOM

38

HANDWRITING

P p

Trace

P P p p

Copy

READING

Read, then draw.

I am big.
I am grey.
I have a trunk.

What am I?

_____

ENGLISH

Write the correct word.

1. We can _____ to school. (ran, run)

2. _____ like to sing. (Us, We)

3. I like _____ friends. (me, my)

4. Matthew _____ a black dog. (have, has)

Child's Name	Parent's Signature

SPACE

Draw a stack of 10 bricks.

MEASUREMENT

Draw a blue kite on the longer string. Draw a patterned kite on the shorter.

NUMBER

Draw 11 raindrops. Trace the numerals.

READING

Read the story "Cinderella".

1. What did Cinderella do at home?

_____

2. Where did Cinderella go?

_____

3. What did Cinderella lose?

_____

4. Who was your favourite in the story?

HANDWRITING

K k

Trace

K K k k

Copy

_____

WORD SEARCH

Find the mystery word.

1. Write the 4th letter in *clock*.
2. Write the 3rd letter in *write*.
3. Write the 2nd letter in *ink*.
4. Write the 1st letter in *dawn*.
5. Write the 5th letter in *rhyme*.
6. Write the 6th letter in *summer*.
7. Write the 3rd letter in *are*.
8. Write the 1st letter in *little*.
9. Write the 5th letter in *little*.
10. Write the 2nd letter in *mad*.

_1_ _2_ _3_ _4_ _5_ _6_ _7_ _8_ _9_ _10_

ENGLISH

Write the sentences. Remember to put spaces between the words.

1. Theclockisonthewall.

_____

2. Thechildrenareplayingontheswings.

_____

3. Thesunisgoingbehindacloud.

_____

Child's Name	Parent's Signature

SPACE

Draw 12 petals on the flower. Trace the numerals.

12 12

MEASUREMENT

Colour the things that will fit inside the treasure chest.

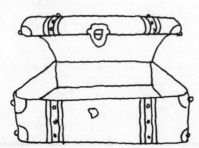

NUMBER

Complete these addition sums.

3 + 0 = _____

2 + 2 = _____

7 + 1 = _____

6 + 0 = _____

5 + 3 = _____

10 + 0 = _____

1 + 8 = _____

4 + 6 = _____

SPELLING

Write a list of **ch** words. The pictures will help you to begin.

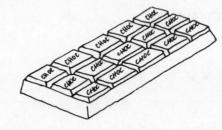

_____ _____ _____ _____

_____ _____ _____ _____

_____ _____ _____ _____

HANDWRITING

R r

Trace

R R R r r

Copy

WORDS

Write the two smaller words from each long word.

1. rockcake

_____ _____

2. birthday

_____ _____

3. policeman

_____ _____

4. moonbeam

_____ _____

WRITING

Write what you think each person is saying.

Child's Name	Parent's Signature

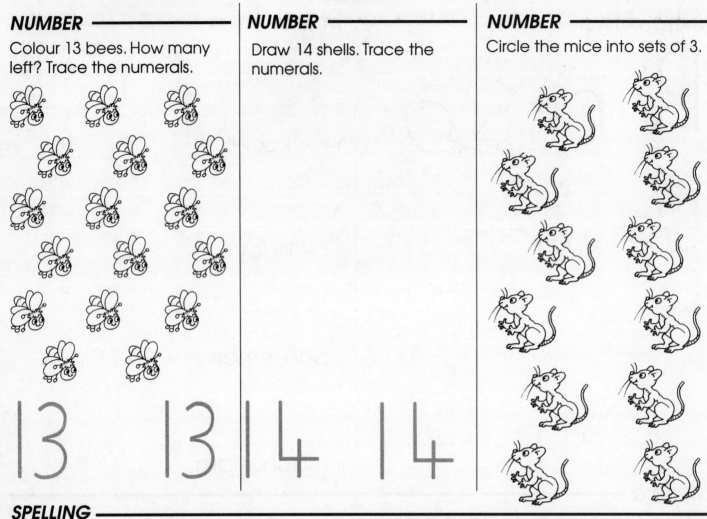

NUMBER

Colour 13 bees. How many left? Trace the numerals.

NUMBER

Draw 14 shells. Trace the numerals.

NUMBER

Circle the mice into sets of 3.

SPELLING

Write each word and draw a picture. Include as many of the things as you can.

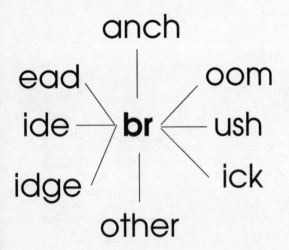

anch

ead

oom

ide — **br** — ush

idge

ick

other

_____

_____   _____   _____

_____   _____   _____

44

HANDWRITING

F f

Trace

F F f f

Copy

_____

READING

Draw lines to join the words that rhyme (sound the same).

big	rub
sad	bed
log	hid
tub	dog
lid	fig
red	dad

WRITING

Keep a diary for 5 days. Write about something you did each day.

Monday _____

_____

Tuesday _____

_____

Wednesday _____

_____

Thursday _____

_____

Friday _____

_____

Child's Name	Parent's Signature

45

Unit 22

NUMBER

Join the dots. Trace the numerals below.

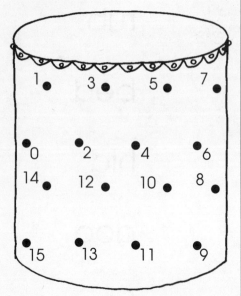

SPACE

Draw a horse under the shade of the tree.

MONEY

Put a **5p** coin and a **50p** coin under this page. Shade over with a pencil to see what happens.

SPELLING

Write the names that go with each picture.

| crown | crab | crayon | cry |

46

HANDWRITING

S s

Trace

S S s s

Copy

_____

READING

Read, then draw.

I have 8 legs.
I live in a web.

What am I?

MORE READING

Answer the questions after reading the party invitation.

Hi!
My name
is Sam and I
will be 8
years old.
Please come
to my party at
2 Martin Avenue
on Saturday 4th
January from
3pm to 5pm.

1. Who is having a party?

_____

2. How old is Sam going to be?

_____

3. Where is the party?

_____

4. What time does the party start?

_____

Child's Name

Parent's Signature

SPACE

Draw 16 stripes on the tiger. Trace the numerals.

16   16

MEASUREMENT

Colour the clown with the wider smile.

NUMBER

Colour 17 balloons. How many left? Trace the numerals.

17   17

SPELLING

Write **dr** in front of these letters. Draw a picture for each word.

___ ___ um   ___ ___ agon   ___ ___ ink

___ ___ eam   ___ ___ ess   ___ ___ ip

HANDWRITING

V v

Trace

V V v v

Copy

STORY WRITING

Finish the story.

A long time ago _____

_____

_____

_____

_____

_____

_____

_____

ENGLISH

Address an envelope to a friend. Remember to put capital letters in the right places.

1st

_____

_____

_____

Child's Name	*Parent's Signature*

SPACE

Draw a lighthouse **on the rocks** and a boat in **front of the rocks**.

MEASUREMENT

Cover a table with books.

How many does it take? _____

Colour the vase that will hold the most water.

NUMBER

Fill in the blanks with shapes and numerals.

◯◯◯ + _____ = ◯◯◯◯◯◯

$3 + \text{\_\_\_} = 5$

△△△△△ + _____ = △△△△△△△

$5 + \text{\_\_\_} = 7$

SPELLING

Colour the **pr** words.

50

Unit 24

HANDWRITING

W w

Trace

W W w

Copy

_____

READING

Write **yes** or **no** to these questions.

1. Can a duck fly? _____

2. Is water dry? _____

3. Do cats have fur? _____

4. Can a snake hop? _____

5. Do sharks have legs? _____

6. Can dogs bark? _____

7. Do children play? _____

WRITING

Write a letter to a friend.

Dear _____ ,

_____

_____

_____

_____

_____

Child's Name	Parent's Signature

51

NUMBER

Colour the greatest number of items.

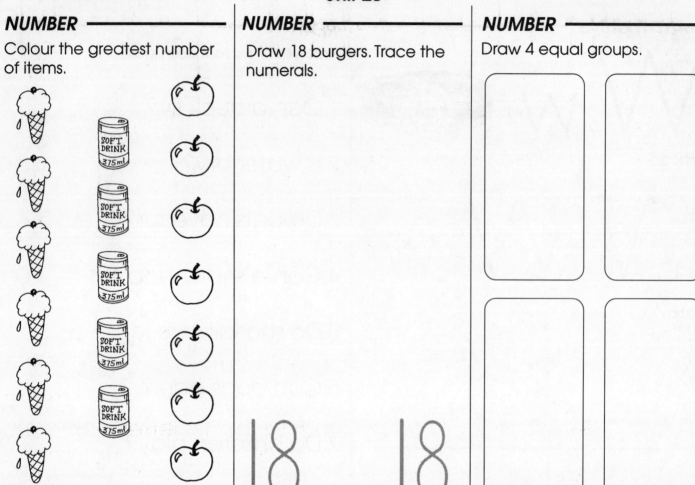

NUMBER

Draw 18 burgers. Trace the numerals.

NUMBER

Draw 4 equal groups.

SPELLING

Help Jack and Jill make some "**ill**" words on their way up and down the hill.

m s p t w k h b d f

__ ill

__ ill   __ ill   __ ill   __ ill

__ ill   __ ill   __ ill   __ ill   __ ill

HANDWRITING

 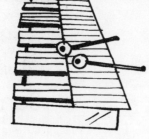

Trace

Copy

WORD BUILDING

Make one word from two smaller words.

pan + cake = _____

hand + bag = _____

wind + mill = _____

pop + corn = _____

READING AND WRITING

Read a book, then write a book review below.

Title _____

Author _____

Illustrator _____

What did you like **best** about the book? _____

_____

_____

What did you like **least** about it? _____

_____

Child's Name	*Parent's Signature*

Unit 26

SPACE ———————————

Draw a beach ball blown up.

TIME ———————————

Name 3 summer months.

1. _____

2. _____

3. _____

Draw a summer picture.

TIME ———————————

Keep a weather chart for one week. Draw pictures.

Sunday	
Monday	
Tuesday	
Wednesday	
Thursday	
Friday	
Saturday	

SPELLING ———————————

Fill the wall with "**all**" words.

m   st   w   t   b   c   f   h

___ all	___ all	___ all
	___ all	___ all
___ all	___ ___ all	___ all

54

HANDWRITING

Z z

Trace

Z Z z z

Copy

_____

ENGLISH

Unjumble these sentences.

1. is pretty. My doll

_____

2. school. go to I

_____

3. and sister I a brother. have

_____

MORE ENGLISH

Punctuate these sentences then rewrite them.

1. will you be my friend

_____

2. can scott ben and katy come to my house

_____

3. what did you do today

_____

Child's Name	Parent's Signature

55

MONEY - COINS

Name the coin by the shape and size.

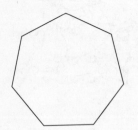

_____ pence

_____ pence

_____ pence

MONEY - NOTES

Colour the notes correctly.

SPELLING

Write the **ell** words in the shells.

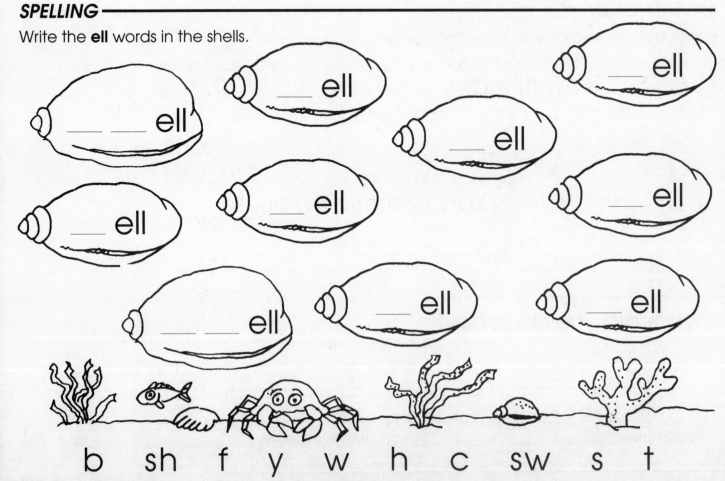

b   sh   f   y   w   h   c   sw   s   t

HANDWRITING

Trace the capital letters.

A B C D E F G H I

J K L M N O P Q R

S T U V W X Y Z

READING

Look at the picture and answer the questions.

1. How many hippos altogether? _____

2. How many hippos with black spots? _____

3. How many hippos with stars on them? _____

4. How many are facing to the right? _____

5. How many are facing to the left? _____

Child's Name	Parent's Signature

57

Unit 28

SPACE —————————

Match the names to the shapes.

MEASUREMENT —————————

How many sides do I have?

NUMBER —————————

Draw 19 stars. Trace the numerals.

cone

cylinder

cube

pyramid

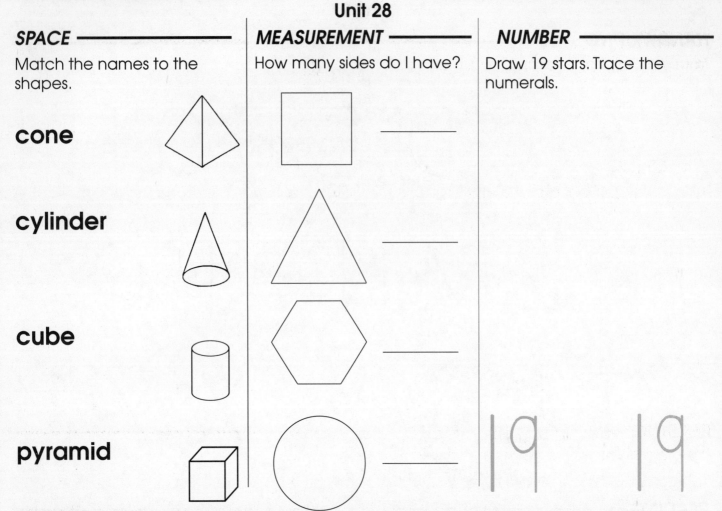

ENGLISH —————————————————————————

Add an **s** to each of these words and write the new word. Draw a picture of any two animals.

1 dog   2 _____

1 cat   2 _____

1 rabbit   2 _____

1 bird   2 _____

1 horse   2 _____

1 goat   2 _____

58

WRITING

Write your first name and your surname (last name).

_____

Practise writing your name 3 more times.

_____

_____

_____

READING

Draw a plan of your classroom. Label as much as you can.

Child's Name	Parent's Signature

SPACE

Draw the shadow of the tree.

MEASUREMENT

How many egg cups of water are needed to fill a cup?

_____ egg cups

How many tea cups of water are needed to fill your kettle?

_____ tea cups

You must ask an adult to help you.

NUMBER

How many more eggs are there than plates?

_____

How many more coins than money boxes?

_____

READING

Draw a **jeep** in a **deep** hole. Put a **sheep** in the back. Write three more **eep** words.

HANDWRITING

Trace then copy.

Bats are nocturnal animals. They come out at night.

_____

_____

READING - RESEARCH

Read, then answer the questions.

Bats are the only mammals that can fly. There are many kinds of bats. Most bats eat insects.

1. When do bats come out?

_____

2. What do bats eat?

_____

3. Can bats fly?

_____

Child's Name	Parent's Signature

SPACE

Draw a shape with 3 sides.

Draw a shape with 4 sides.

Draw a shape with 6 sides.

NUMBER

Trace the numerals 1-19.

1 2 3 4
5 6 7 8
9 10 11
12 13 14
15 16 17
18 19

NUMBER

Draw:

4 groups of 6

5 groups of 2

SPELLING - WORD BUILDING

Write the **ing** words.

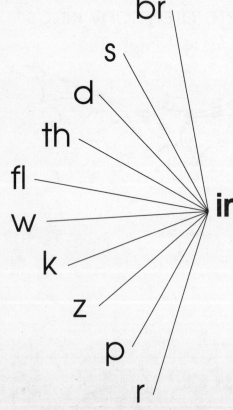

br
s
d
th
fl
w
k
z
p
r

ing

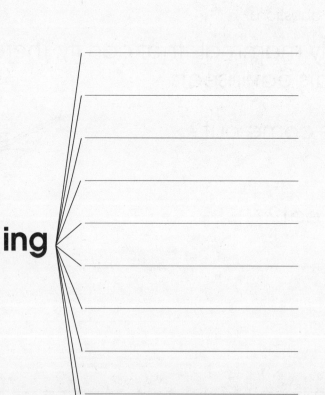

HANDWRITING

Trace then copy.

Wild rabbits are very
common animals.

_____

_____

READING - RESEARCH

Read, then answer the questions.

Rabbits are mammals. They live in underground tunnels.
They can hop and run very fast. They have long ears.

1. Where do rabbits live?

_____

2. Do rabbits have short or long ears?

_____

Child's Name	Parent's Signature

UNIT 1   page 4

Space:
Parent
Measurement:
Dinosaur taller than tree
Number:
6 more suns
Spelling:
cat, pat, hat, bat, mat, sat, rat, fat
e.g. The fat cat sat on the mat

UNIT 1   page 5

Handwriting:
Parent
Reading:
Hand holding ice lolly and plate under it.
10 Letter i L
English:
Parent

UNIT 2   page 6

Space:
Parent
Measurement:
Coloured: hedgehog, pineapple, toothbrush
Circled: mirror, leaf
Number:
6   5
Spelling:
jet, bet, wet, let, net, set, get, pet, vet

UNIT 2   page 7

Handwriting:
Parent

Reading:
 Parent: Duck on pond, frog on bank

English:
tree, frog, duck, pond

UNIT 3   page 8

Space:
Parent/Teacher
Measurement:
Parent/Teacher - full bottle, half filled glass
Number:
3
Spelling:
e.g. knit, sit, bit, fit, hit, kit, lit (answers may vary)

UNIT 3   page 9

Handwriting:
Parent
Word Search:

d	k	i	w		n
b	o	a	t		o
i	o	s	a	m	
g	h	s	i	f	

Reading:
1. Sam   2. Saturday   3. Happy

UNIT 4   page 10

Number:
5 red, 2 yellow, 1 orange, and 4 purple
Money:
Parent/Teacher
Measurement:

Spelling:
pot, cot, dot, got, hot, lot, not, spot, jot

UNIT 4   page 11

Handwriting:
Parent

Reading
Parent

English:
Parent

UNIT 5   page 12

Space:	Measurement:	Number:
★ ☐	Sunday	2
✳ ○	Monday	3
△ ○	Tuesday	
☐	Wednesday	
○	Thursday	
✳ ○	Friday	**Spelling:**
△ ☐	Saturday	cut, but, hut, jut, nut, rut, put

UNIT 5   page 13

Handwriting:
Parent
Alphabet:
a b c d e f g h i j k l m
n o p q r s t u v w x y z
Reading:
bus   garden   cup   years
flat   begin   there   chill

UNIT 6   page 14

Space:
left: blue   middle: green
Measurement:
Parent
Number:
2x20 pence coins red, 1x50 pence coin green
Spelling:
tap, map, wrap, rap, gap, cap nap, zap, lap, sap

UNIT 6   page 15

Handwriting:
parent
Alphabet:
1. baby 2. cake 3. egg 4. frog 5. kite
6. man
Reading:

runner   girl   sleep   playing
   reading   draw   ball
   read   girl skipping
   play
   run   boy
sleeping   skip   drawing

UNIT 7   page 16

Space:
Parent
Measurement:
Parent
Number:
8 clocks
Word Building:
pat pet pit put pot
sat set sit shut shot (answers will vary)

UNIT 7   page 17

Handwriting:
Parent
Spelling:
Circled: axe, day, van, goat, sack, had, walk, watch
Reading and Writing:
apple,   igloo,   box,   zebra
web   gate   kite   snake

UNIT 8   page 18

Reading:
tree   crab
Measurement:
Pattern on the curved ribbon
Number:
Lines to bucket, gloves and hat
Spelling:
dip, hip, lip, nip, pip, rip, sip, tip, whip

UNIT 8   page 19

Handwriting:
Parent
Alphabet:
1. a b c d e f g   2. t u v w x y z
3. l m n o p q   4. a b c d e
5. f g h i j k
English:
1. Josh went swimming in the lake.
2. Ellen and Jake had a birthday.
3. On Sunday Sam went to a party

UNIT 9   page 20

Space: **Measurement:**   **Number:**
Colour inside shape   ★★★★★
Parent/Teacher   ★★★★★

Spelling:
can, ban, fan, man, pan, ran, tan, van
(answers will vary)

UNIT 9   page 21

Handwriting:
Parent

Reading:
homework

English:
Parent

UNIT 10   page 22

Space:
○   ◇   (answers may vary)
Measurement:
Flower under 1st tree and bird in tall tree
Number:
5 + 2 = 7   6 + 3 = 9
Spelling:
den, hen, pen, men, ten, when

UNIT 10   page 23

Handwriting:
Parent

Reading:
Draw boy with red car and green train

Writing:
Parent

UNIT 11   page 24

Space:

Measurement:
Parent

Number:
3 hearts left
2 flowers left

Spelling:
fin, pin, win, spin, bin, thin, chin
Drawing: Thin pin in the bottom of a bin

UNIT 11   page 25

Handwriting:
Parent
Reading:
lipstick   sandcastle
English:
1. Tie a hook on your line.
2. Put bait on your hook.
3. Throw line into water.
4. Wait until you feel a bite.

UNIT 12   page 26

Measurement:
Book on right
1. Clean teeth   2. Brush hair
3. Get dressed (answers will vary)
Number:
5   5   2 rows of 5 = 10
Parent
Spelling:
bun, fun, run, nun, gun, sun

UNIT 12   page 27

Handwriting:
Parent
Alphabet:
1. Monday, Sunday, Tuesday, Wednesday
2. cat, dog, fish, horse
3. beach, crab, sand, water
English
1. Glen, Tim and Dylan went sailing.
2. Andrew loves to play with his toys.
3. My friends Kathy and Lara came to play.

UNIT 13   page 28

Measurement:
Answers will vary depending on length of pencil

Number:
Parent

Spelling:
Parent

UNIT 13   page 29

Handwriting:
Parent

Reading:
Parent

Alphabet:
1. book   2. car   3. glove   4. shoe

UNIT 14   page 30

Space:
Answers will vary depending on model

Measurement:
Parent (answers will vary)

Number:
2
0
1

Spelling:
cloud, clown, clover, clock, clap

UNIT 14   page 31

Handwriting:
Parent

Alphabet:
1. b   2. u   3. q   4. x   5. n
Parent

English:
Parent

UNIT 15   page 32

Space:

Measurement:
Bottom bucket

Number
0 1 2 3 4 5
6 7 8 9 10

Spelling:
sled, slide, slippers, sleeve, sleep (answers may vary)

UNIT 15   page 33

Handwriting:
Parent
Word Building:
enormous, large, huge, gigantic, vast, tremendous (many other words possible)
Reading:
1. A big castle   2. On Saturday
3. Red
Parent

UNIT 16	**page 34**

Space:
Circle: boat, cork, leaf
Measurement:
2 circles coloured   2 or more circles
Number:
7 8 9 9 8 10
Spelling:
plane, plant, plate, planet

UNIT 16	**page 35**

Handwriting:
Parent

Word Building:
e.g. hot, happy, help, holiday, hippo

English:
Parent

UNIT 17	**page 36**

Measurement:
1. Eating dinner   2. Cleaning room
3. Making your bed (answers will vary)
Number:
6   4   1   1   5   6
Spelling:
Coloured: shirt, shoes, socks, skipping rope, skates,
scarf, shorts, sunglasses, spade, shell, sheep, star,
sailing boat

UNIT 17	**page 37**

Handwriting:
Parent
Reading:
m(at)   in(to)   (fit)   (this)
(tray)   po(nd)   (shop)   m(eat)
English:
1. Humpty Dumpty sat on a wall.
2. I am going to a party.
3. Amy is watching television.

UNIT 18	**page 38**

Number:
4 groups of 6   5 groups of 5
Measurement:
3 apples in each basket
Spelling:
1. three   2. thin   3. thick   4. throat
5. they   6. thunder
(Th)ere once were (th)ree (th)in friends. (Th)ey loved to
play in (th)e rain. (Th)eo did not like (th)e (th)under.

UNIT 18	**page 38**

Handwriting:
Parent

Reading:
Picture of an elephant
Elephant

English:
1. run   2. we   3. my   4. has

UNIT 19	**page 40**

Space: **Measurement:**   **Number:**
          2 kites   Parent
          blue on right
          patterned on left
          (answers will vary)

Reading:
1. She cleaned and cooked.
2. She went to the ball.
3. Cinderella lost a glass slipper.
4. Parent

UNIT 19	**page 41**

Handwriting:
Parent
Word Search:
Cinderella
English:
1. The clock is on the wall.
2. The children are playing on the swings.
3. The sun is going behind a cloud.

UNIT 20	**page 42**

Space: **Measurement:**   **Number**
          gold   3, 4, 8, 6
          crown   8, 10, 9, 10
          goblet

Spelling:
chair, chips, chocolate, chimney, church, chin,
chop, chum etc. (answers will vary)

UNIT 20	**page 43**

Handwriting:
Parent

Words:
1. rock   cake   2. birth   day
3. police   man   4. moon   beam

Writing:
Parent

UNIT 21	**page 44**	UNIT 21	**page 45**

Number:
4 bees are not coloured

Number:
Parent

Number:
4 sets of 3 mice

Spelling:
branch, broom, brush, brick, brother, bridge, bride, bread

Handwriting:
Parent

Reading:
big - fig   sad - dad   log - dog
tub - rub   lid - hid red - bed

Writing:
Parent

UNIT 22	**page 46**	UNIT 22	**page 47**

Number:
Parent

Space:
Drawn: horse on left hand side of tree

Money:
Parent
crab, crayon, crown, cry

Handwriting:
Parent

Reading:
Picture of a spider
Spider

More Reading:
1. Sam   2. 8 years old
3. 2 Martin Avenue   4. 3 pm

UNIT 23	**page 48**	UNIT 23	**page 49**

Space:
Parent

Measurement:
Bottom clown coloured

Number:
8 balloons are not coloured

Spelling:
drum, dragon, drink, dream, dress, drip

Handwriting:
Parent

Story Writing:
Parent

English:
Parent

UNIT 24	**page 50**	UNIT 24	**page 51**

Space:
Drawn: lighthouse on rocks, boat in front

Measurement:
Answer will vary according to size of books and table
Bottom vase coloured

Number:
○ ○ 2   △ △   2

Spelling:
Coloured: pram, prince, princess, presents

Handwriting:
Parent

Reading:
1. Yes 2. No 3. Yes 4. No 5. No
6. Yes 7. Yes

Writing:
Parent

UNIT 25	**page 52**	UNIT 25	**page 53**

Number:
Apples coloured

Number:
Parent

Number:
Parent

Spelling:
mill,   sill,   pill,   till,   will,
kill,   hill,   bill,   dill,   fill

Handwriting:
Parent

Word Building:
pancake, handbag, windmill, popcorn

Reading and Writing:
Parent

UNIT 26 — page 54

Space:

○

Time:
June
July
August (answers may vary)
Summer picture

Time:
Parent

Spelling:
mall, stall, wall, tall, ball, call, fall, hall

UNIT 26 — page 55

Handwriting:
Parent
English:
1. My doll is pretty.   2. I go to school.
3. I have a brother and sister.
More English:
1. Will you be my friend?
2. Can Scott, Ben and Katy come to my   house?
3. What did you do today?

UNIT 27 — page 56

Money-Coins:
50 pence   5 pence   2 pence

Money - Notes:
Parent

Spelling:
bell, shell, fell, yell, well, hell, cell, swell, sell, tell

UNIT 27 — page 57

Handwriting:
Parent

Reading:
1. 10, 2. 1, 3. 3, 4. 5, 5. 5

UNIT 28 — page 58

Space:
cone
cylinder
cube
pyramid

Measurement:
4
3
6
0

Number:
★ ★ ★ ★ ★
★ ★ ★ ★ ★
★ ★ ★ ★ ★
★ ★ ★ ★

English:
2 dogs, 2 cats, 2 rabbits, 2 birds, 2 horses, 2 goats
Parent

UNIT 28 — page 59

Writing:
Parent

Reading:
Parent

UNIT 29 — page 60

Space:
Shadow below tree and to right
Measurement:
Parent (answers will vary)
Number:
2   2
Reading:
Parent

UNIT 29 — page 61

Handwriting:
Parent

Reading - Research
1. At night.
2. Insects.
3. Yes.

UNIT 30 — page 62

Space:

△
▭
⬡

Number:
Parent

Number:
Parent

Spelling - Word Building:
bring, sing, ding, thing, fling, wing, king, zing, ping, ring

UNIT 30 — page 63

Handwriting:
Parent

Reading - Research:
1. In underground tunnels.
2. Long.

69

Sales, Marketing and Distribution to the book trade

Unit 350, Glenfield Park Site 2, Blakewater Road, Blackburn, Lancashire BB1 5QH
Telephone: 01254 696768 Fax: 01254 697060

The following titles published by Nightingale Press can be ordered direct from Pegasus Distribution Limited: -

ISBN	Title	Price	Quantity	
1 875288 69 4	Leap Ahead with Maths Book 1	£2.99		_____
1 875288 70 8	Leap Ahead with Maths Book 2	£2.99		_____
1 875288 71 6	Leap Ahead with Maths Book 3	£2.99		_____
1 875288 72 4	Leap Ahead with Maths Book 4	£2.99		_____
1 875288 73 2	Leap Ahead with Maths Book 5	£2.99		_____
1 875288 74 0	Leap Ahead with Maths Book 6	£2.99		_____
1 875288 75 9	Leap Ahead with Maths Book 7	£2.99		_____
1 875288 65 1	Pre-School Maths	£2.99		_____
1 875288 66 X	Pre-School Reading	£2.99		_____
1 875288 67 8	Pre-School Writing	£2.99		_____
1 875288 77 5	Computer Classroom CD-Rom Level 1	£29.95 (inc VAT)		_____
1 875288 78 3	Computer Classroom CD-Rom Level 2	£29.95 (inc VAT)		_____
1 875288 79 1	Computer Classroom CD-Rom Level 3	£29.95 (inc VAT)		_____
1 875288 80 5	Computer Classroom CD-Rom Level 4	£29.95 (inc VAT)		_____
1 876052 36 8	Reading Made Easy Book 1	£3.99	(July 97)	_____
1 876052 37 6	Reading Made Easy Book 2	£3.99	(July 97)	_____
1 876052 38 4	Reading Made Easy Book 3	£3.99	(July 97)	_____
1 876052 39 2	Reading Made Easy Book 4	£3.99	(July 97)	_____
1 876052 30 9	Maths Made Easy CD-Rom Level 1	£29.95 (inc VAT)	(Aug 97)	_____
1 876052 31 7	Maths Made Easy CD-Rom Level 2	£29.95 (inc VAT)	(Aug 97)	_____
1 875288 54 6	Homework Tonight Book 1	£3.99	(Sept 97)	_____
1 875288 55 4	Homework Tonight Book 2	£3.99	(Sept 97)	_____
1 875288 56 2	Homework Tonight Book 3	£3.99	(Sept 97)	_____
1 875288 57 0	Homework Tonight Book 4	£3.99	(Sept 97)	_____
1 875288 58 9	Homework Tonight Book 5	£3.99	(Sept 97)	_____
1 875288 59 7	Homework Tonight Book 6	£3.99	(Sept 97)	_____

- -

Name _____

Address _____

_____

_____

_____ Postcode _____

To: **Pegasus Distribution Ltd, Unit 350, Glenfield Park Site 2, Blakewater Road, Blackburn, BB1 5QH**

I enclose a cheque for £ _____ (inc P + P) made payable to Pegasus Distribution Limited.
Add 50p per book up to maximum of £3.50 for P+P
Add £1.50 per CD-Rom for P+P

Please allow 21 days for delivery. If you have any queries or require any further information please telephone Pegasus on 01254-696768

Certificate of
Achievement

This is to certify that

_____

has successfully completed the activities in this
Homework Tonight book

signed:_____

dated: _____

Well
Done!